Math in Focus®

Singapore Math®
by Marshall Cavendish®

Student Book
Kindergarten Ⓐ
Part 1

Author
Dr. Pamela Sharpe

U.S. Consultants
Andy Clark and Patsy F. Kanter

Houghton
Mifflin
Harcourt

© 2009 Marshall Cavendish International (Singapore) Private Limited
© 2014 Marshall Cavendish Education Pte Ltd

Published by Marshall Cavendish Education
Times Centre, 1 New Industrial Road, Singapore 536196
Customer Service Hotline: (65) 6213 9688
US Office Tel: (1-914) 332 8888 | Fax: (1-914) 332 8882
E-mail: cs@mceducation.com
Website: www.mceducation.com

Distributed by
Houghton Mifflin Harcourt
222 Berkeley Street
Boston, MA 02116
Tel: 617-351-5000
Website: www.hmheducation.com/mathinfocus

First published 2009

Math in Focus® Kindergarten A Part 1
ISBN 978-0-669-01097-8

Printed in Singapore

18 19 20   1401   22 21 20
4500812919   B C D E

Contents

Lesson 1 **Finding a Match: All About 1 and 2**

Recite.

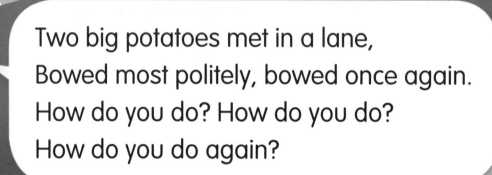

Two big potatoes met in a lane,
Bowed most politely, bowed once again.
How do you do? How do you do?
How do you do again?

Two tall green beans met in a lane,
Bowed most politely, bowed once again.
How do you do? How do you do?
How do you do again?

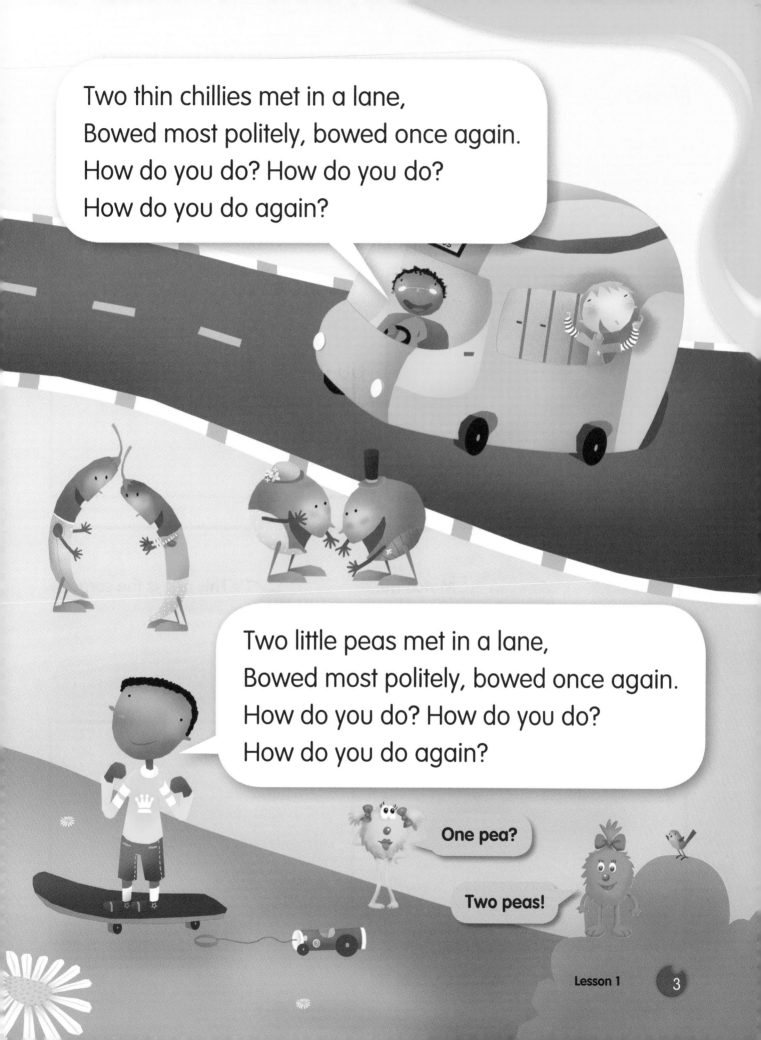

Match.

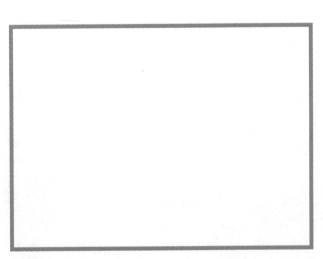

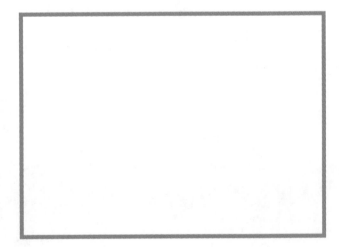

Match.

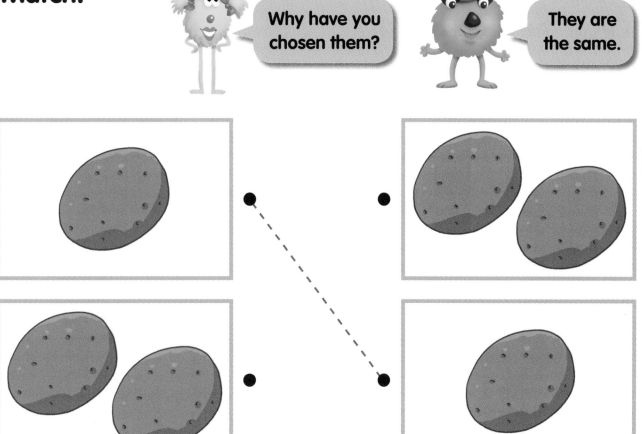

Trace.

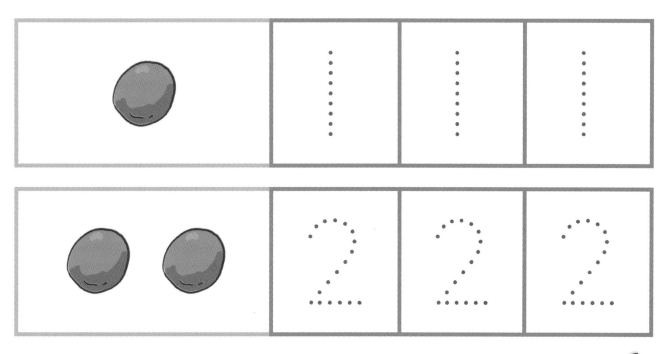

Circle the groups of 2.

Draw the same object.

This is the same.

Write the same number.

Draw an object that is not the same.

This is not the same.

Write a number that is not the same.

Color the same object.

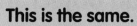
This is the same.

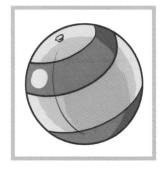   

Count and write.

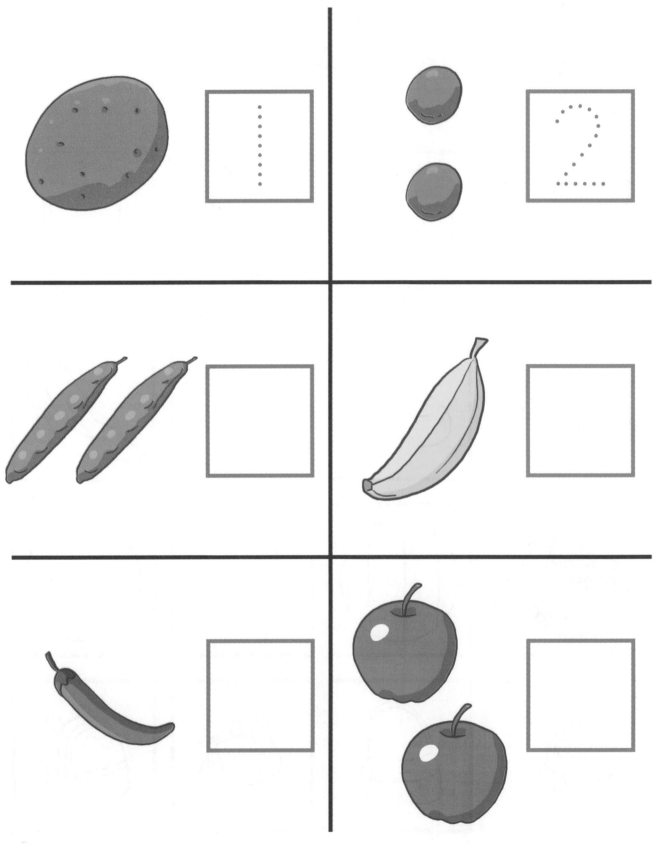

What is different? Point and say.

Match.

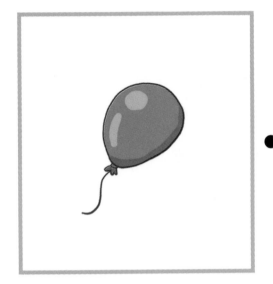 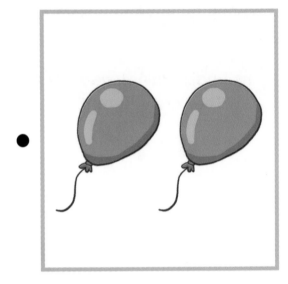

 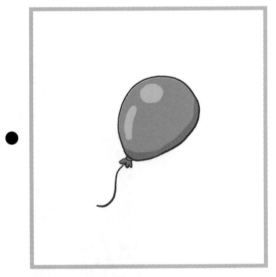

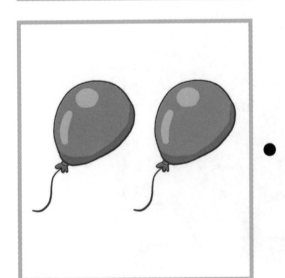 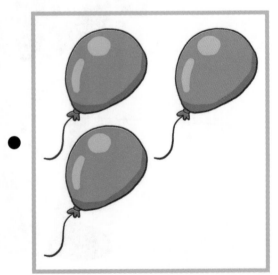

Trace.

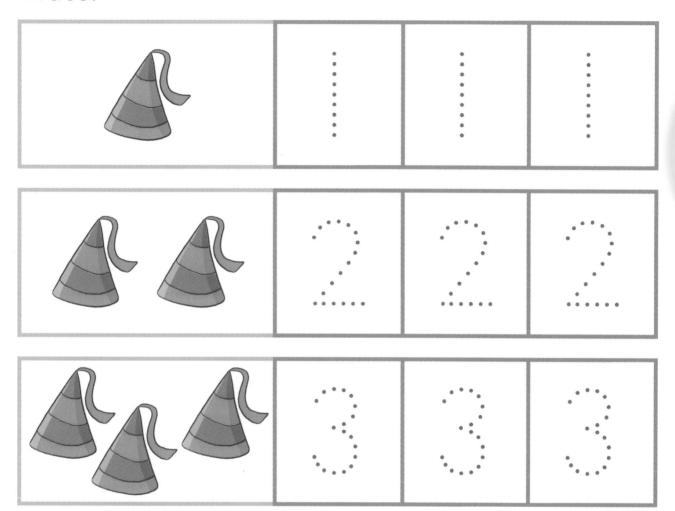

Look and say.

Count and write.

Look and say.

Papa Bear is big.
He has a black bag.

Look and say.

Baby Bear has green shoes. Mama Bear has pink shoes.

Papa Bear is big. Baby Bear is small.

Match.

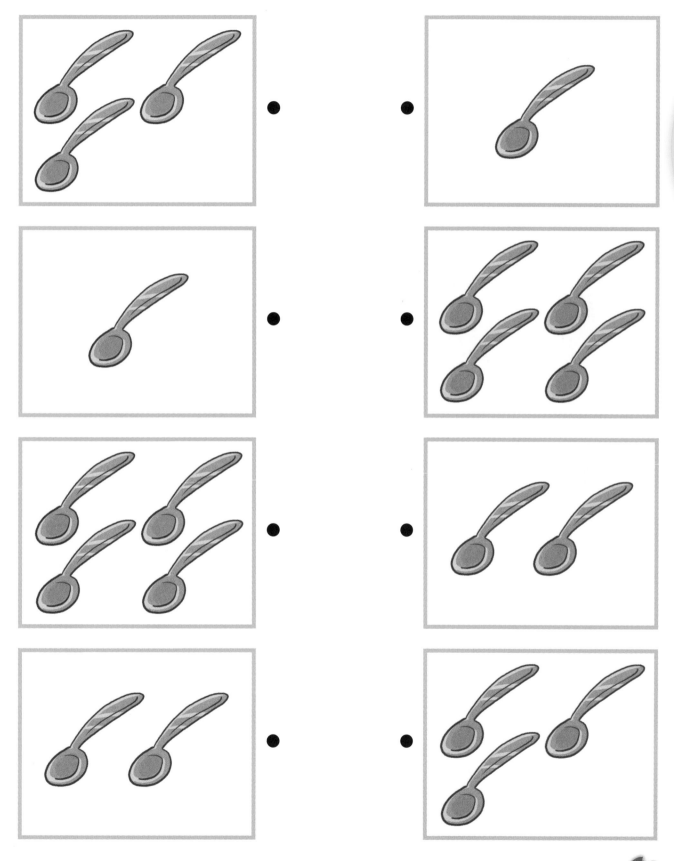

Trace.

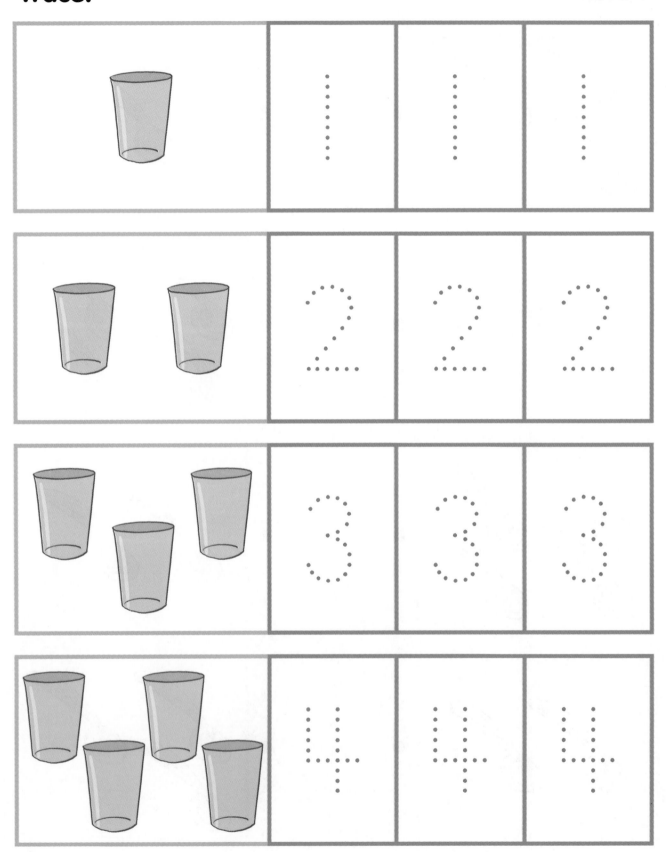

Count and write.

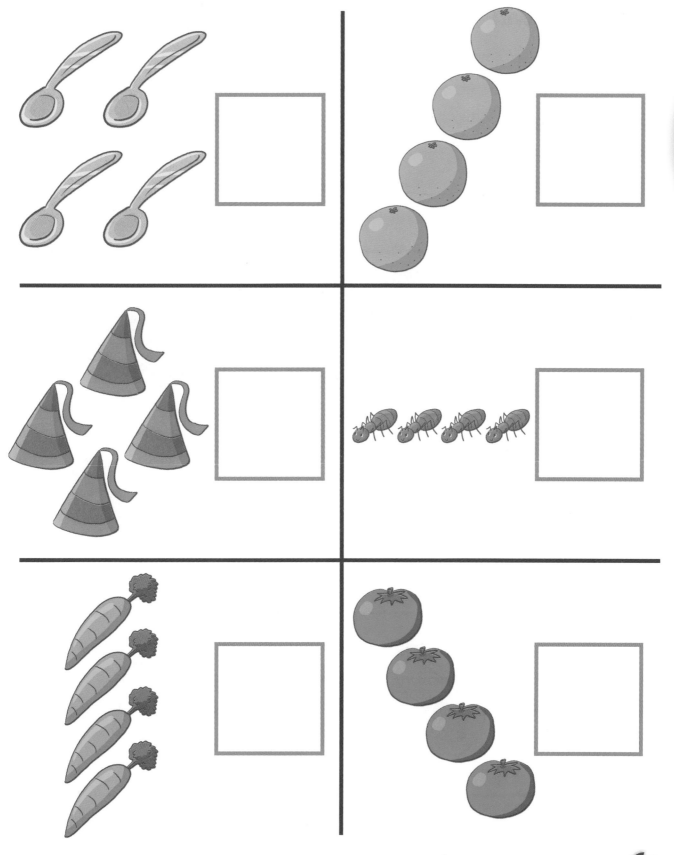

Look and win.

Look at the picture your teacher is holding up.

Look and say.

Draw a pretend animal.

My animal has ...

Match.

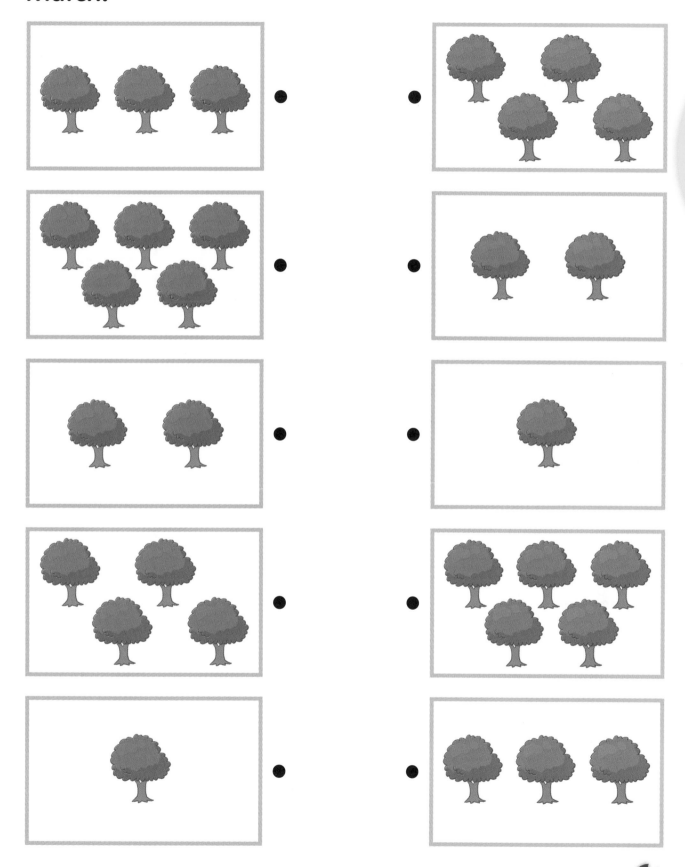

Trace.

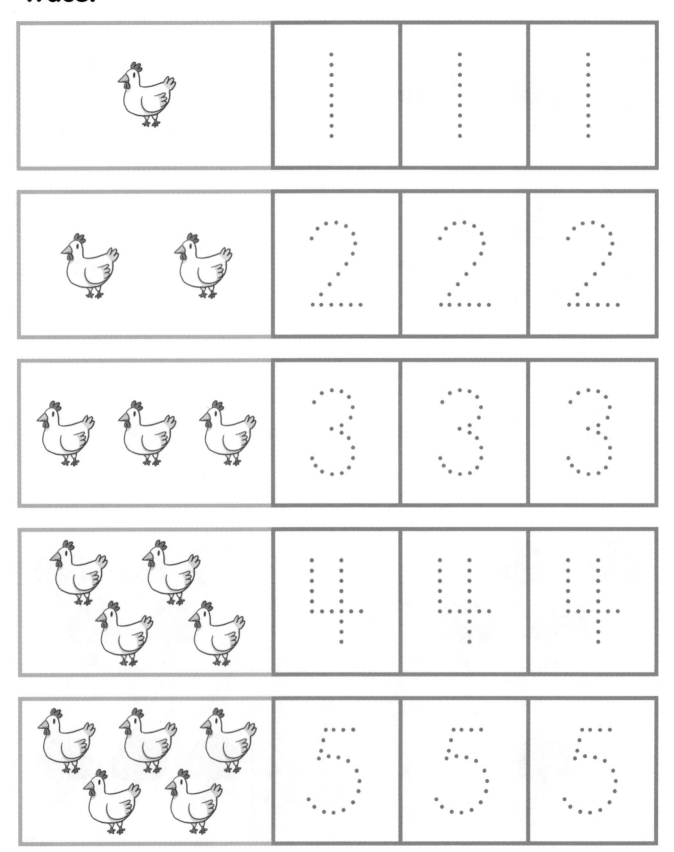

Count and write.

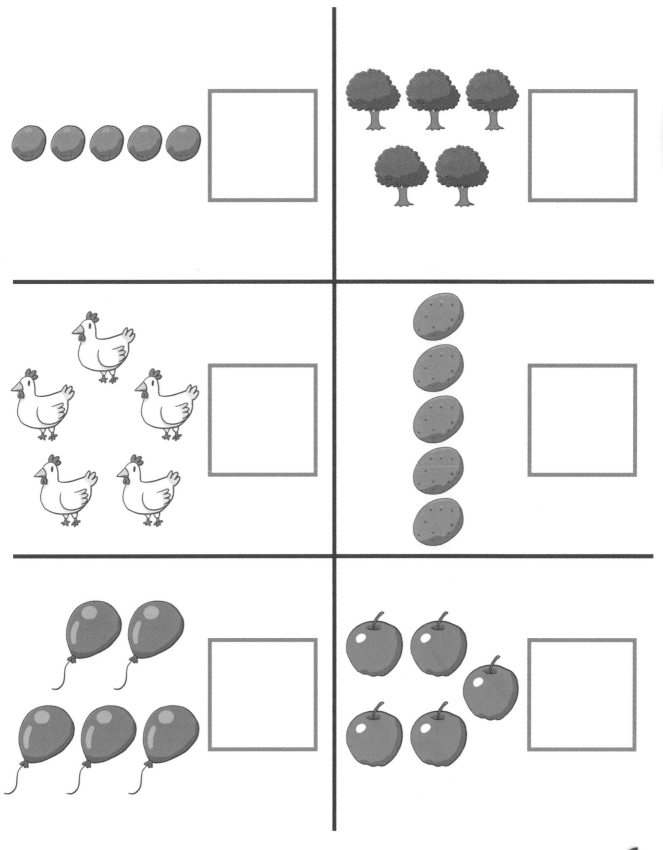

Lesson 6 A Few Differences
Circle the differences.

What is different?

things are different!

Lesson 1 **Pairing Sets: All About 6**

Sing.

One red engine,
One red engine puffing
down the track.
One red engine puffing,
puffing back.

Two red engines,
Two red engines puffing
down the track.
Two red engines puffing,
puffing back.

Three red engines,

Three red engines puffing down the track.

Three red engines puffing, puffing back.

Four red engines,

Four red engines puffing down the track.

Four red engines puffing, puffing back.

Five red engines,
Five red engines puffing down the track.
Five red engines puffing, puffing back.

Six red engines,
Six red engines puffing down the track.
Six red engines puffing, puffing back.

Match.

Match me.

This one is the same.

Match.

 •

•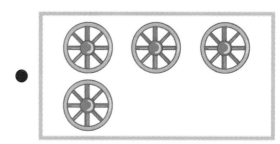

 •

•

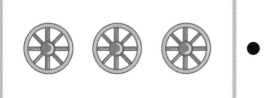 •

•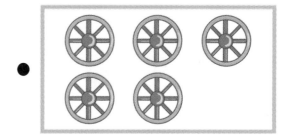

 •

•

 •

•

 •

•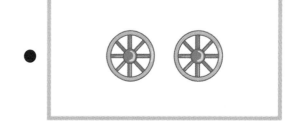

Draw.

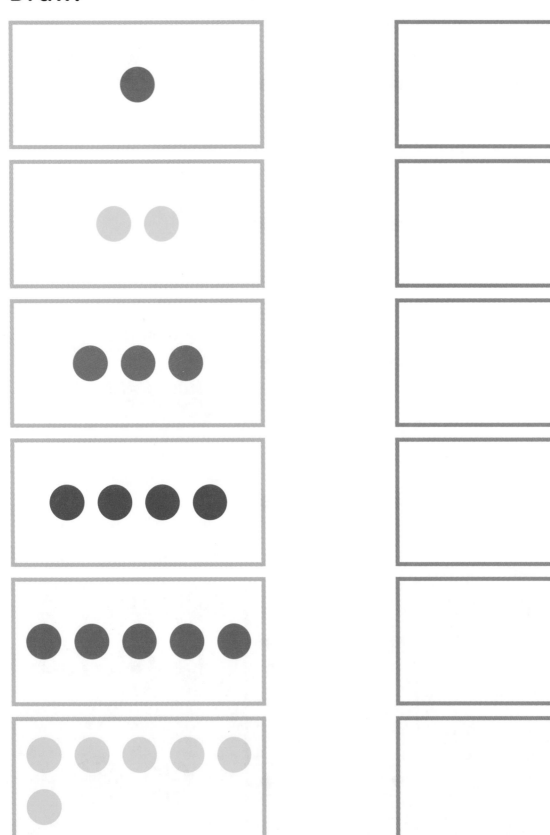

Trace.

🚩	1	1	1
🚩🚩	2	2	2
🚩🚩🚩	3	3	3
🚩🚩🚩🚩	4	4	4
🚩🚩🚩🚩🚩	5	5	5
🚩🚩🚩🚩🚩🚩	6	6	6

Sing.

Here is the beehive.

Where are the bees?

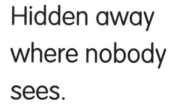
Hidden away where nobody sees.

Circle the groups of seven bees.

Match.

Draw.

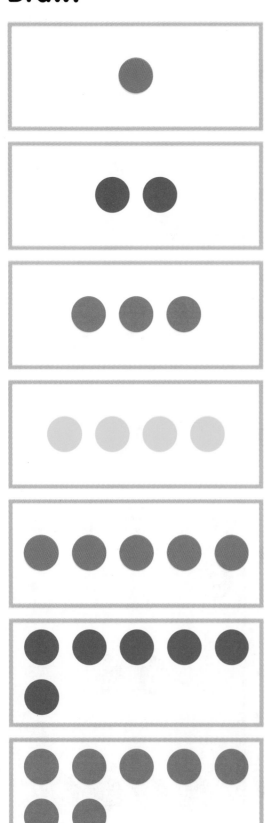

Trace.

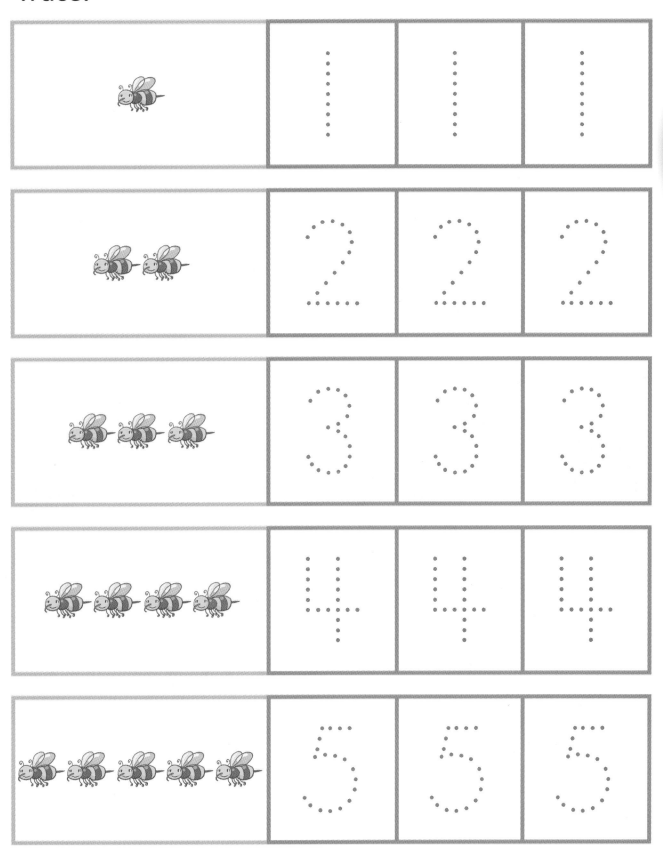

Trace.

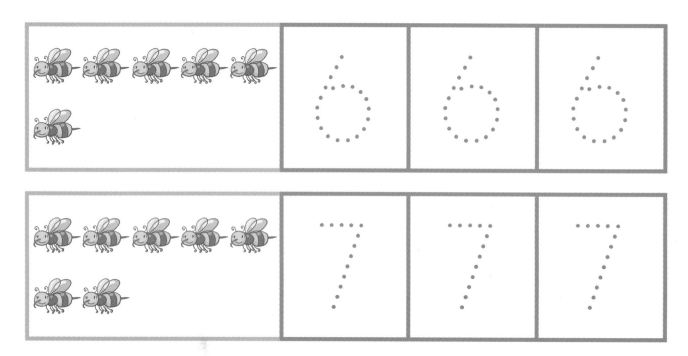

Look and say.

Count and write.

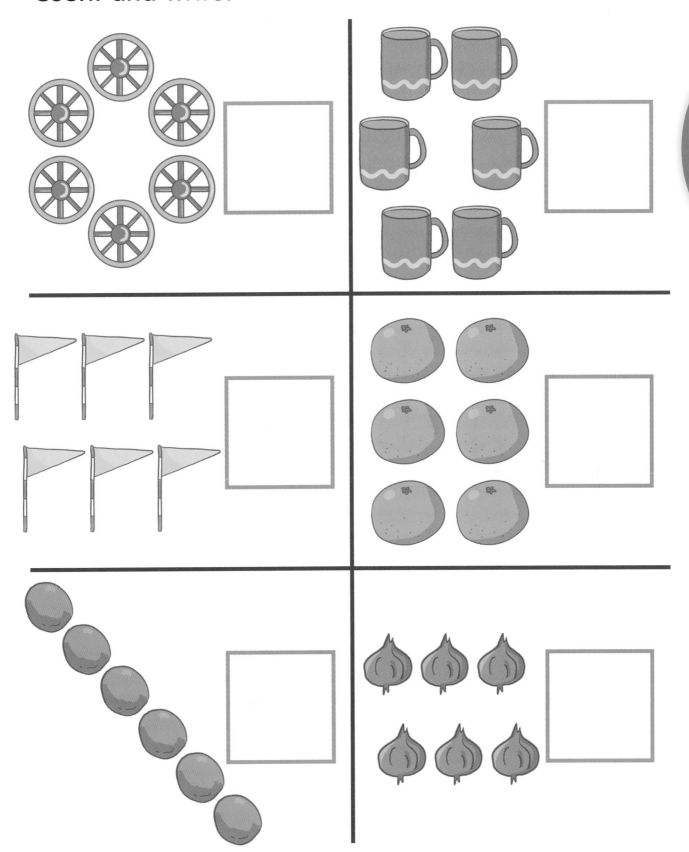

Count and write.

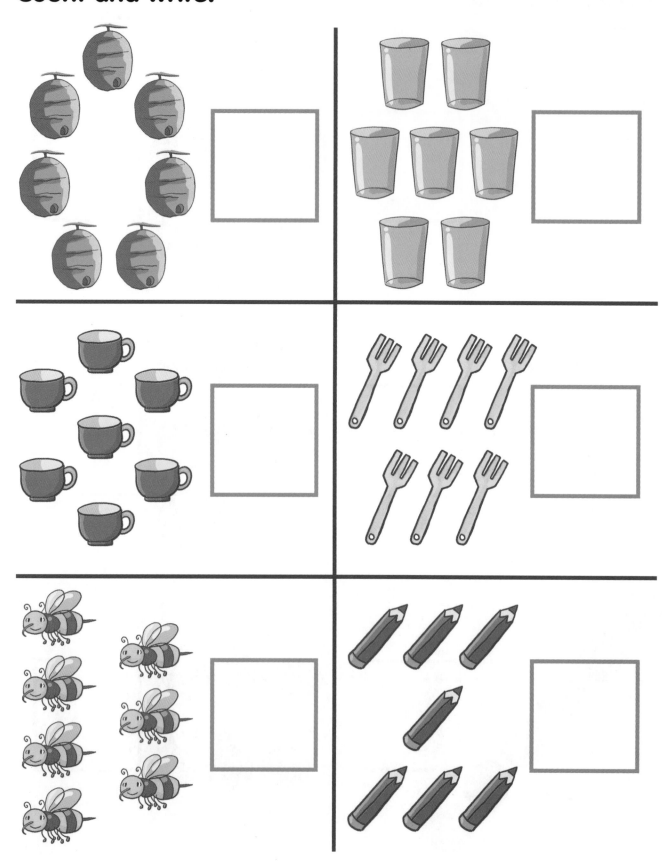

What is missing?
Complete the set.

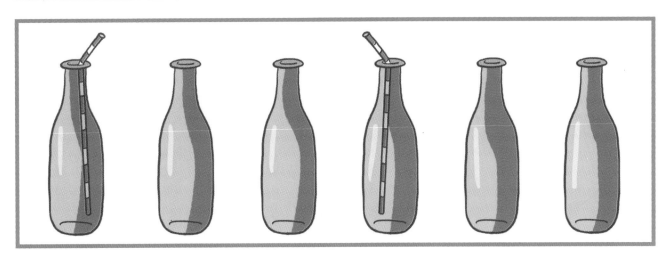

Color.

5   6   7   8

Draw.

Match.

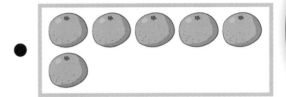

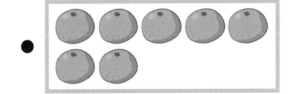

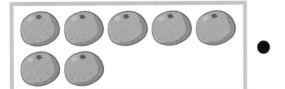

Draw.

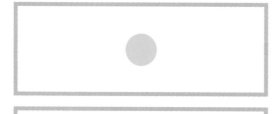

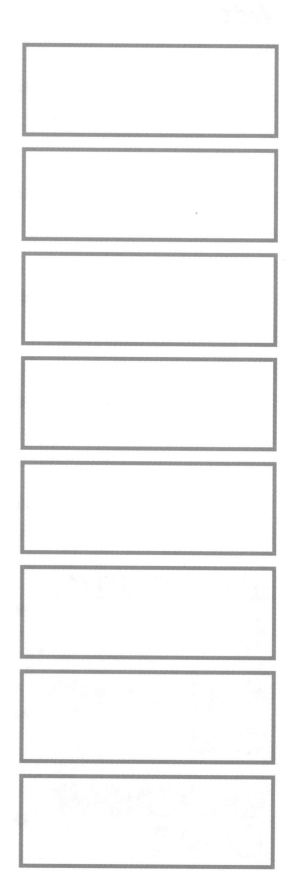

Trace.

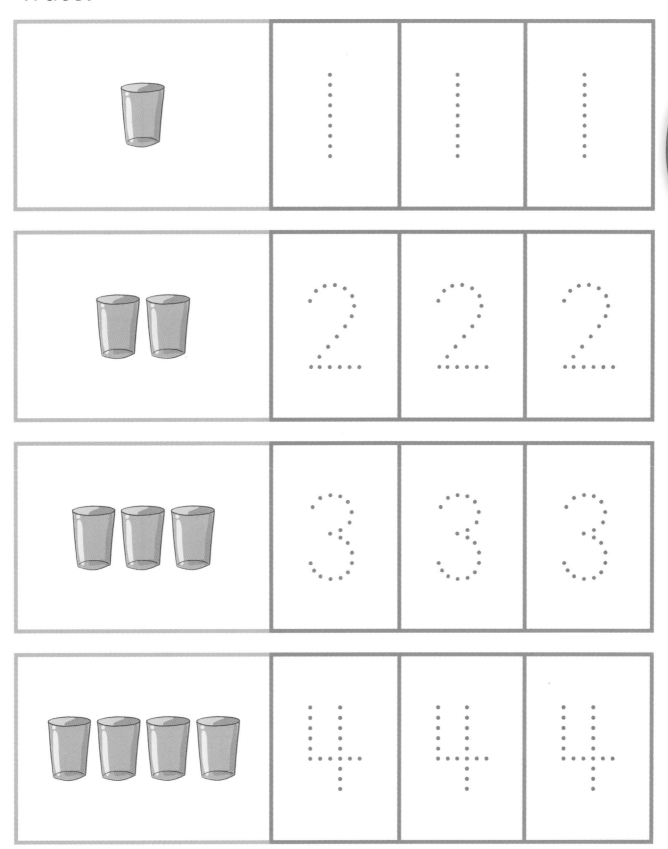

Trace.

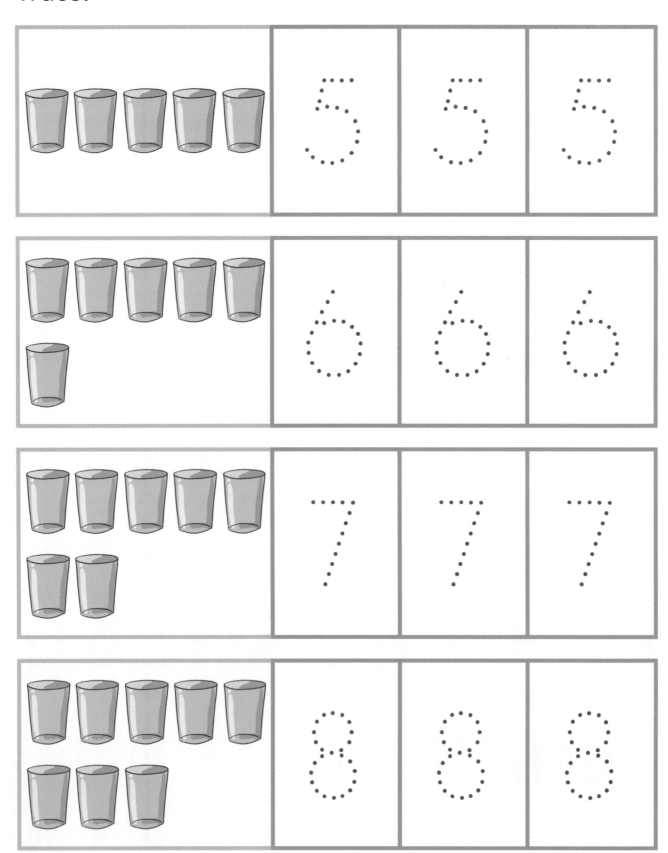

Lesson 4 Numbers 0 to 9
Circle the group of 9 players.

Write the number.

Write the missing numbers.

9

Stop.

6

9

Lesson 4 57

Match.

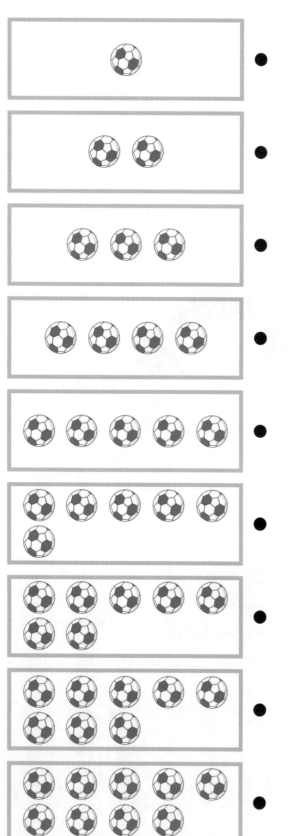
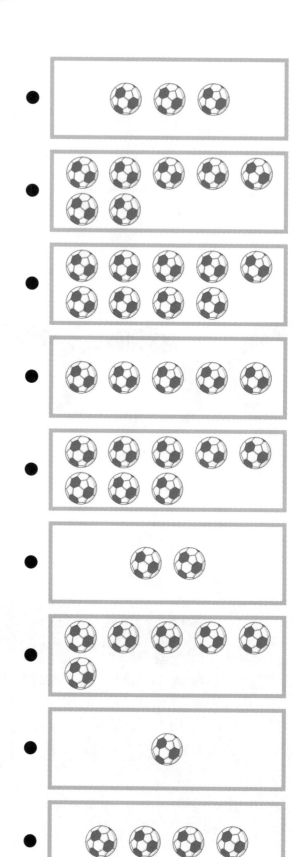

Draw.

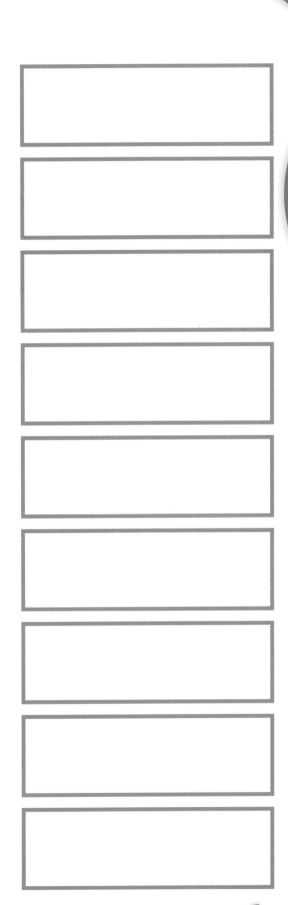

Trace.

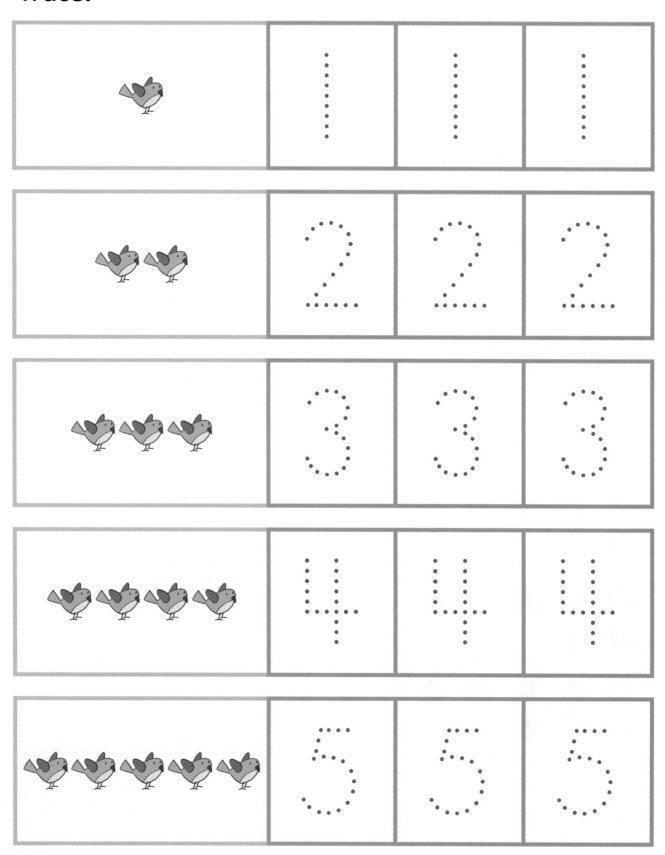

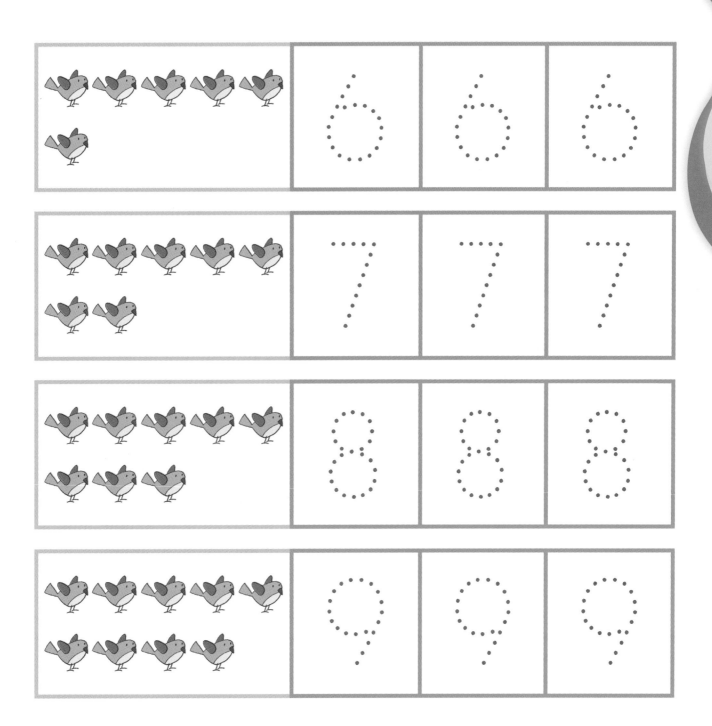

Circle, count, and write.

There is cheese for 6 mice.

How many mice will be hungry? _____

3 boys have coats.

How many boys will be cold? _____

There are 6 egg holders.

How many eggs are needed to fill all the egg holders? _____

WORK MAT

0
1
2
3
4
5
6
7
8
9

0
1
2
3
4
5
6
7
8
9

Trace.

	0	0	0
ı	1	1	1
ıı	2	2	2
ııı	3	3	3
ıııı	4	4	4

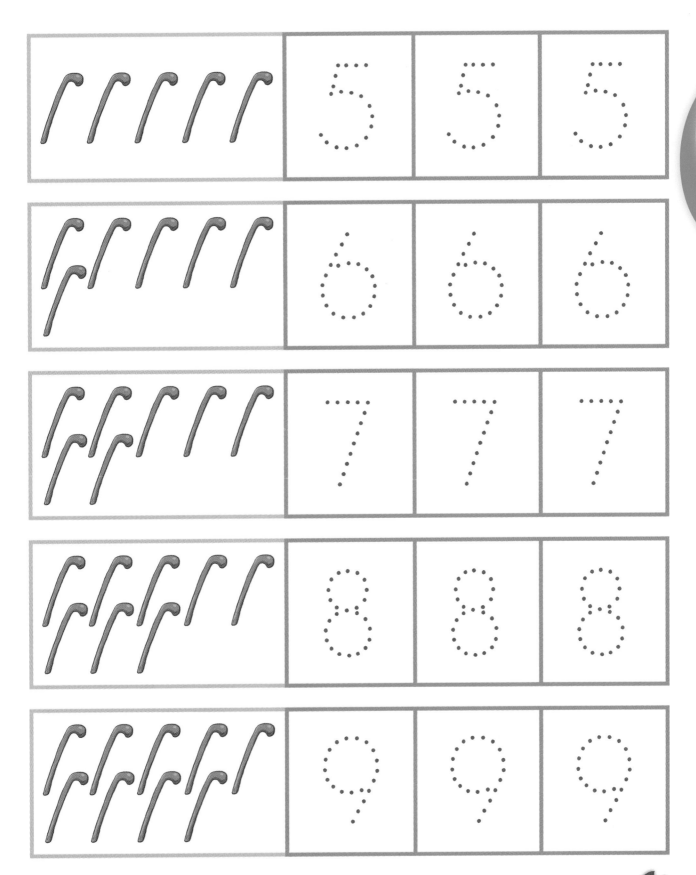

Count and write.

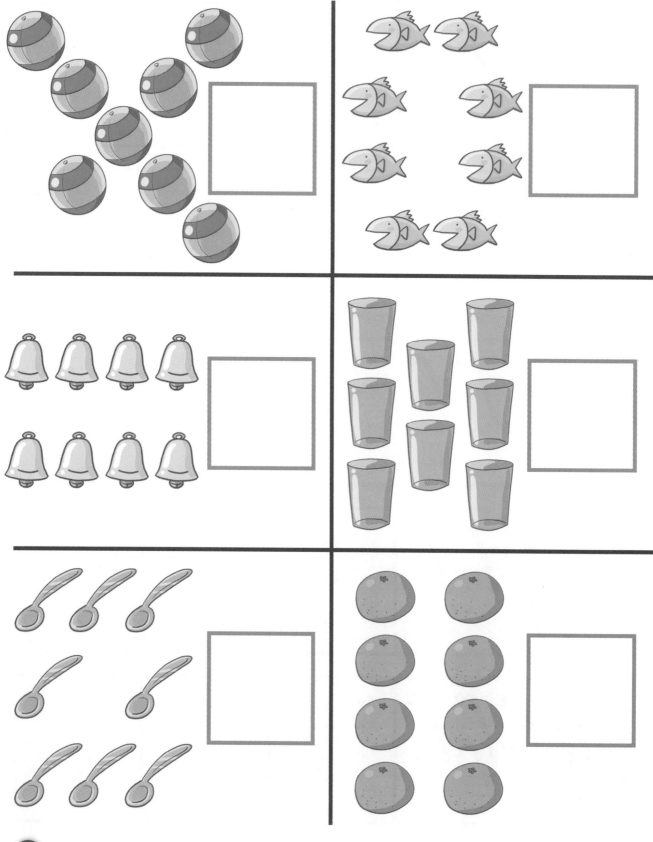

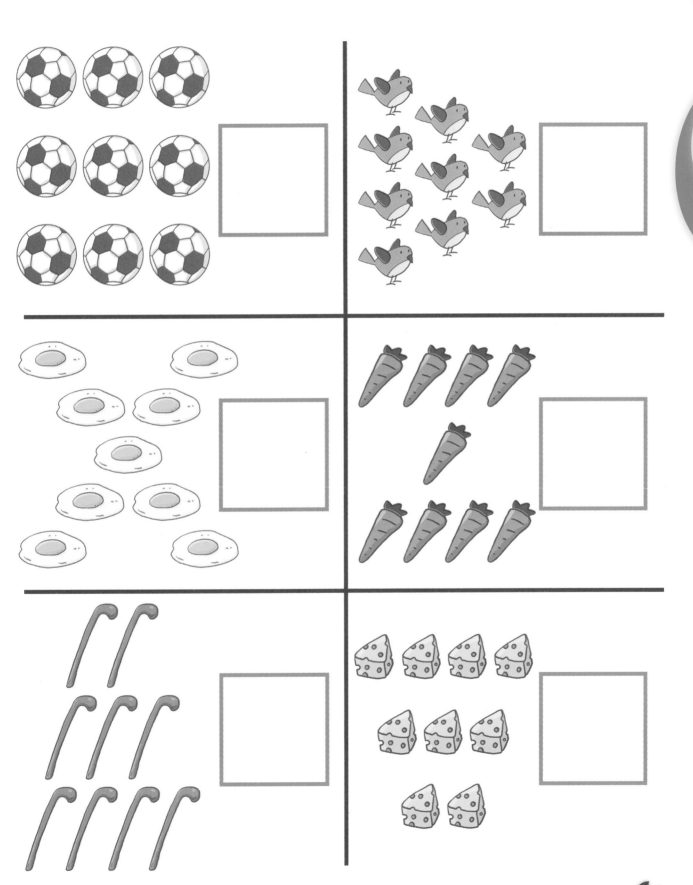